License to Cook Arizona Style
Revised and Expanded
Recipes reflecting the bounty of the land and the cultures of th

Compiled by Dianna Stevens Cover design and line drawings by Diane F
Associate Editors: Dorothy Crum, Dwayne M. and Joan Liffring-Zug Bourret, Melind
Maureen Patterson, and Liz Rolfsmeier

Penfield
BOOKS

The Compiler

Dianna Stevens is a journalism graduate of Northwestern University and a freelance writer. She lives in Charlotte, North Carolina, with her husband, Trey, and children Alexandra, MacPherson, and Annabella.

Acknowledgments

Thanks to individual contributors listed with their recipes, as well as Hanje Richard, Treasure Publications; Sandal English, author of *Fruits of the Desert;* Filter Press; and Joyce McCullough Peters, Tucson, Arizona. Special thanks to the *Jalapeño Cafe,* which exists only on the Internet, and to GourMedia & M.F. Munday, Tucson, Arizona, for permission to reprint *Tables of Difference* recipes.

ISBN 1-932043-00-4   Copyright © 1999 Penfield Press Copyright © 2002 Penfield Books

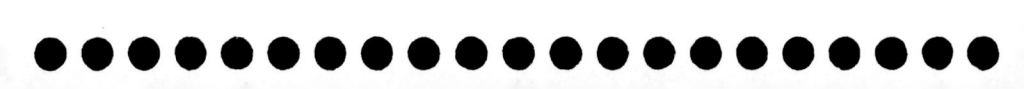

Contents

- 4 -

The Joy of Southwestern Cuisine

"The food is hot and full flavored and so visual with the warm colors of chiles, corn, and cheeses. Every dish is a treat to both the taste buds and the eyes. Over the years, I've tried French, Italian, Chinese, Vietnamese, Cuban, Southern, New American, and many other types of cooking, but I always return to my favorite, and that is Southwestern cuisine.

"I am a dyed-in-the-wool 'foodie,' a walking repository of recipes, food lore, and cooking tips. I started cooking when I was seven or eight years old, and I've never stopped. I've baked, boiled, and fried my way through hundreds of cookbooks. Once, I was so engrossed in following a *Joy of Cooking* recipe that I laid

the open cookbook on a hot burner of the stove. I may be the only person alive who has ever cooked the *Joy of Cooking*.

"In my spare time, I maintain a website, the Jalapeño Café, which is devoted to the culture and recipes of the Southwest."

—Carol Blakely

Editor's Note: Carol's recipes appear on pages 40, 52, 81, and 83 of this book.

Arizona

Awe-inspiring. Beguiling. Majestic. Stark. Spectacular! All capture the essence of Arizona. From solemn deserts colored like a child's paint box to piney mountains, ancient dwellings to glittering cities, grand canyons to giant cacti, Arizona is a land of stark contrast and startling beauty.

Saguaro Cactus Blossoms
Arizona State Flower

Our 48th state, Arizona joined the nation in 1912 after generations of Spanish and Mexican influence. Known as the Grand Canyon state, Arizona has much more to boast about than one of the seven natural wonders of the world and hot, hot temperatures.

The Grand Canyon, formed at the dawn of time, is a mile deep and fascinating to millions of visitors each year. Contrasting the canyon's dramatic depths is the South Rim, where the largest Ponderosa Pine forest in the world carpets the way to the San Francisco Peaks, sacred to the Hopis and Navajos.

The western border, shared with California, Nevada, and Mexico, is often referred to as the West Coast in honor of its spectacular lakes and rivers. Water sports abound in this part of the state, where you can pass through all five climate zones in one day and even see the original London Bridge at Lake Havasu City. Granite block by block, the bridge was brought to Lake Havasu City in 1968 when London outgrew it.

In southern Arizona, bordering Mexico, ghost towns offer a glimpse of

Arizona's Wild West days while thoroughly modern cowboys work the range and ranches. There's the OK Corral in Tombstone, made famous by the Earps and Clantons. Giant saguaro cacti grow up to fifty feet tall in the desert. The city of Tucson is a vacation mecca right in the middle of a desert valley.

Arizona is the sixth-largest state, and roughly a fourth of it is home to American-Indian reservations; it has the third-largest American-Indian population in the country after Oklahoma and California. Although the Navajos are the largest tribe, fourteen tribes live in Arizona. Indian country, the northeast corner of the state, also boasts the Petrified Forest, the famed Painted Desert, and the ancient cliff dwellings at Canyon de Chelly.

In addition to the American Indians of Arizona, many Arizonans claim

Mexican descent. And there are folks who have migrated from other states, lured by the warm sun and growing cities—some staying the winter, some all year.

Although much of Arizona is desert, it produces a surprising array of foods. Ranch lands support the beef and dairy industry. Crop lands are irrigated and offer a variety of fruits and vegetables. Arizona is famous for its citrus fruits, lettuce, pecans, chiles, corn, and tomatoes. There are sunflower seeds, pistachios, walnuts, beans, berries, olives, peaches, pears, pomegranates—more bounty than you would ever expect to squeeze from a desert.

Copper and gold mining, popular in the Wild West days, are still chief industries in Arizona. The state's motto is "God Enriches." One trip to Arizona will make you nod in agreement.

Beverages

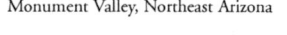

Monument Valley, Northeast Arizona

Grapefruit Punch

8 cups grapefruit juice
2 cups tangerine juice
1 pint ginger ale

Lime slices, for garnish
Mint, for garnish

Thoroughly chill all ingredients. Combine citrus juices with ginger ale in a punch bowl. Add cracked ice. Garnish with lime slices and mint. Makes 24 half-cup servings.

—From *Fruits of the Desert*, by Sandal English, Filter Press

Honey of a Peach Shake

American Dairy Association, Dairy Council of Arizona, Inc.

1 cup milk
2 large ripe peaches, peeled and
  sliced, or 2 cups frozen peach
  slices, partially thawed

2 tablespoons honey
1 tablespoon lemon juice
1/2 teaspoon vanilla
4 scoops vanilla ice cream

In a blender, combine milk, peaches, honey, lemon juice, and vanilla. Blend until combined. Add ice cream and blend until smooth. Pour into 2 tall glasses.

Lemon-Lime Shake

American Dairy Association, Dairy Council of Arizona, Inc.

1 cup milk
1/2 cup frozen lemonade
   concentrate
4 scoops vanilla ice cream

2 scoops lime sherbet
Whipped cream
Grated lemon and lime peel, for
   garnish

Place milk, lemonade concentrate, and ice cream in a blender; mix until combined. Add sherbet; blend until smooth. Pour into 2 tall glasses. Top with whipped cream and lemon and lime peel, if desired.

Fresh Orangeade

Sunkist Growers

1 cup fresh squeezed lemon juice
3/4 to 1 cup sugar

4 cups fresh squeezed orange juice
Ice cubes

In a large pitcher, combine lemon juice and sugar; stir to dissolve sugar. Add orange juice. Serve over ice cubes. Makes 5-1/2 cups.

Old-Fashioned Lemonade

1 cup sugar   1 quart cold water
1 cup fresh lemon juice   Lemon slices

In a pitcher, dissolve sugar in lemon juice. Stir in the water. Chill and serve over ice with lemon slices for garnish, if desired. Makes 6 cups.

Sangria

Hummingbird

1 orange
1 lemon, thinly sliced
Juice of 1 lemon
1/2 cup sugar
2 bottles of Burgundy
1 quart club soda

Peel orange, reserving peel. Squeeze orange into a large bowl. Add orange peel, lemon slices, and juice, then sugar and Burgundy. Stir well; chill thoroughly. Strain into a punch bowl. Add the club soda and serve. Makes 12 servings.

● ● ● ● ● ● ● ● ● ● ● ● ● ● ● ● ● ● ● ●

Cafe Con Leche

6 cups hot, strong coffee   2 cups milk, warm
1/4 cup brown sugar   4 cinnamon sticks

Combine coffee and brown sugar. Add warm milk and pour into 4 mugs. Add a cinnamon stick to each mug.

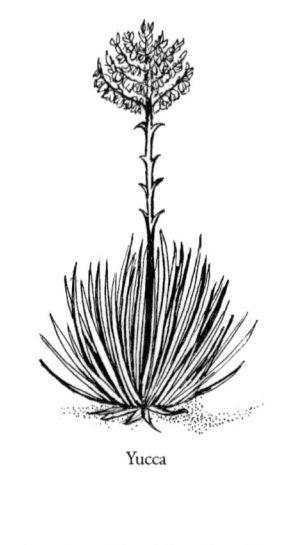

Yucca

Dips, Salsas, and "Hot Stuff"

Jalapeño Cheese Dip

1 pound Monterey Jack cheese
   with jalapeños, grated
8 ounces sour cream
1/4 cup mayonnaise
1 large garlic clove, pressed

2 ounces chopped pimiento
3 green onions, finely chopped
Sunflower seeds
Tortilla chips

Combine the cheese, sour cream, mayonnaise, and garlic. Bake at 350° for about 20 minutes or in microwave on high for about 10 minutes, stirring occasionally. Remove from oven and mix in pimiento, onion, and sunflower seeds. Bake 5 more minutes or microwave on high for 2 to 3 minutes. Serve warm with tortilla chips.

Nacho Dip

Lois Wiley, Tucson, Arizona

2 cups chili with beans
   (homemade or prepared)
8 ounces cream cheese, softened
2 (2-1/4-ounce) cans green chiles

1 cup shredded Monterey Jack cheese
1 (2-1/4-ounce) can chopped
   black olives

Spread chili in an 8 x 8-inch casserole dish. Spread cream cheese over chili. Scatter drained green chiles over cream cheese and top with shredded cheese and olives. Bake at 350° for about 20 minutes or until cheese bubbles. Serve warm with tortilla chips.

Hot Taco-Bean Dip

1 pound ground beef
1 package taco seasoning mix
1/2 cup water
1 (15-ounce) can refried beans

1 pint sour cream
1-1/4 cups taco sauce
1-1/2 cups grated Cheddar cheese

Brown ground beef in a skillet and add taco seasoning and water. Stir in the beans and heat until warm. Spread mixture in a 9 x 13-inch baking pan. Combine the sour cream and taco sauce and spread this over the meat mixture. Top with the grated cheese. Bake at 350° for 30 minutes or until bubbly. Serve warm with tortilla chips.

Baked Artichoke Dip
Mary Jo Richmond, Mesa, Arizona

1 (15-ounce) can unmarinated
    artichoke hearts
1 cup mayonnaise
1 cup Parmesan cheese

1 (2-1/4-ounce) can chopped
    green chiles
1 cup shredded Mozzarella cheese

Drain and cut artichoke hearts into smaller pieces. Combine artichoke hearts, mayonnaise, Parmesan cheese, and chiles. Spread in an 8 x 8-inch baking dish. Top with shredded cheese and bake at 350° for 15 to 20 minutes.

Guacamole

Claire Bourret, Sun Lakes, Arizona

1/2 cup mayonnaise
1 small tomato, chopped
1 large avocado, peeled and mashed
1/4 cup white onion, minced

1/4 cup green chiles, drained and
chopped
1 tablespoon lemon juice

Combine all ingredients; cover and chill. Makes 2 cups.

Avocado Salsa

4 cups corn kernels
3/4 cup sliced ripe olives
1 medium sweet red pepper, chopped
1 to 2 jalapeños, chopped
1 small onion, chopped
5 cloves garlic, minced
1/3 cup olive or vegetable oil
1/4 cup lemon juice

3 tablespoons cider or white wine vinegar
1 teaspoon dried oregano
1/2 teaspoon salt
1/2 teaspoon pepper
4 medium, ripe avocados
Tortilla chips

In a large bowl, combine corn, olives, red pepper, jalapeño, and onion. Combine garlic, oil, lemon juice, vinegar, oregano, salt, and pepper. Mix well. Pour the vinegar mixture over the corn mixture and toss to coat. Cover and refrigerate overnight. Chop avocados and stir into salsa just before serving. Makes about 6 cups of salsa.

Prehistoric Pottery Design

Red Chile Sauce

8 red chile pods   1 teaspoon salt
5 cloves garlic

Remove stems and seeds from pods. Place in a glass dish and cover with water. Microwave for 10 minutes or until pods are soft. Drain water and rinse pods with cold water. Drain and place pods in a blender with garlic and salt. Pour fresh water into the blender, filling until it is 3/4 full. Blend until smooth; there should be no pieces of pod visible. Add more water for a thinner sauce. Pour sauce into a medium saucepan and simmer on low for 45 minutes. Use sauce on cooked pork, beef, or with any meal.

Stuffed Jalapeños

1/2 pound Colby Jack cheese　　　　　Salt, to taste
12 fresh jalapeño chiles

Slice cheese into small rectangular chunks, about 1-1/2 inches long. You will need 2 pieces of cheese for each chile. Cut jalapeños in half lengthwise; remove seeds. Place them on a foil-lined cookie sheet, smooth side up. Broil 2 to 3 minutes or until tops of chiles begin to char slightly. Remove from oven. Turn chiles over and sprinkle each with salt. Place a chunk of the cheese in each half and return the chiles to the oven until the cheese melts, about 2 to 5 minutes. Serve warm.

Pico de Gallo

A salsa to use for fajitas, a dip, or as an accompaniment to meat or fish. The name in Spanish dictionaries means "beak of the rooster." A popular Southwestern dish.

2 large tomatoes, seeded and diced
1 medium white onion, diced
2 cloves garlic, minced
2/3 cup cucumber, peeled and diced

5 radishes, diced
1/3 cup fresh cilantro leaves, chopped
3 to 4 fresh serrano chiles, seeded,
    very finely chopped

In a medium bowl, combine all the ingredients, adding salt to taste. Refrigerate, covered, at least 1 hour before serving. Makes 3 cups.

Glazed Hot Pecans

Pecans are grown in the middle and high desert areas of Arizona.

1/2 cup water
1/2 cup sugar
2 dried red chiles

1 cup pecan halves
1/4 cup molasses

Preheat oven to 250°. Combine water, sugar, and chiles in a small saucepan. Bring to a boil over high heat. Add pecans and return to boil. Lower heat and simmer 10 minutes. Remove and discard the chiles. Drain pecans and place on a cookie sheet. Bake for 45 minutes, stirring occasionally. Pour baked pecans into a small bowl, stirring in the molasses. Place on a fresh cookie sheet. Bake another 45 minutes until crisp.

Dry Rub

Refrigerate this spicy dry rub on chicken, ribs, or beef the night before grilling.

1 tablespoon ground black pepper
1 tablespoon ground white pepper
1 tablespoon sugar
2 teaspoons ground cayenne chiles
2 tablespoons chili powder
1 tablespoon cumin
1 tablespoon garlic powder

1 tablespoon brown sugar
1 tablespoon ground oregano
4 tablespoons sweet paprika
1 teaspoon dry mustard
1 tablespoon celery salt
1 tablespoon salt

Thoroughly combine all ingredients. Rub mixture into the meat of your choice.

Wrap coated meat tightly in plastic wrap and refrigerate overnight or for at least 8 hours. Store remaining mixture in a jar in the refrigerator or freezer.

Horned Lizard

Cherry Tomato Salsa

2 pints cherry tomatoes
1 large shallot, minced
1 large garlic clove, minced
2 tablespoons minced fresh coriander

1 tablespoon white wine vinegar
2 serrano chiles, seeded and minced
2 teaspoons fresh lime juice
1/4 teaspoon salt

In a food processor, coarsely chop the tomatoes. In a medium bowl, combine the tomatoes and their juice with the shallot, garlic, coriander, vinegar, chiles, lime juice, and salt. Stir well. Cover tightly and refrigerate at least 2 hours before serving. Makes 2-1/2 cups of salsa.

Salsa
Cindy Manternach, Mesa, Arizona

1 (28-ounce) can crushed tomatoes
2 (15-1/2-ounce) cans Mexican
    stewed tomatoes
1 bunch scallions, sliced
1 clove garlic, minced
2 tablespoons minced fresh cilantro
1 tablespoon white wine vinegar

1 to 2 jalapeño chiles, sliced
2 teaspoons fresh lime juice
1/4 teaspoon salt
2 carrots, finely chopped
1 teaspoon lemon pepper
1 teaspoon basil
1 tablespoon sugar

Combine all ingredients and store in the refrigerator. Makes 4 pints.

Picanté Sauce

Use this spicy sauce as a condiment with meats, chips, or eggs.

3 tomatoes, peeled and chopped
3 to 4 tablespoons ground red chiles
1 cup finely chopped onion
1 cup vinegar

1/8 teaspoon oregano
1/8 teaspoon cumin
1/4 teaspoon salt

Combine all ingredients and chill thoroughly. Serves 4.

Salads

White House, Canyon de Chelly National Monument

Topopo

Carol Blakely

This recipe is similar to a chicken salad originally served at a famous Tucson restaurant. One of the cooks saw a volcano while visiting in Mexico and, upon her return to Arizona, created a "topopo" (volcano) in salad form.

6 corn tortillas, fried crisp
1 cup refried beans
1 bunch of leaf lettuce, torn in pieces and dressed with 1/4 cup Italian dressing
3 plum tomatoes, sliced
2 avocados, peeled and sliced

8 ounces longhorn Cheddar cheese, cut in strips
1 bell pepper, cut in strips
3 grilled chicken breasts, cut in thin strips
4 radishes, sliced
1/2 cup ripe olives, sliced

Spread the tortilla with refried beans. Build a mound of dressed lettuce, shaping like a volcano. (One cook packed the lettuce into a large funnel to shape a mound.) Stack tomato, avocado, cheese strips, bell pepper strips, and chicken strips around and over the mound of lettuce as you would build a teepee. Garnish with radish and olive slices. Serve with side dishes of salsa and sour cream.

Lemon Fruit and Chicken Salad
Sunkist Growers

Grated peel of 1/2 lemon
Juice of 1 lemon
1-1/2 tablespoons vegetable oil
1 tablespoon honey
1/4 teaspoon ground ginger

1/4 teaspoon curry powder
1 cup shredded, cooked, light
    chicken meat
1 cup cooked orzo pasta (1/3 cup
    uncooked)

In a large bowl, combine lemon peel and juice, oil, honey, and spices. Stir in remaining ingredients; chill. Serve on salad greens and garnish with lemon wedges and fresh mint, if desired. Makes 6 one-cup servings.

Spicy Grilled Shrimp and Melon Salad

15 dried de arbol chiles
1-1/2 cups olive oil
1 teaspoon salt
2 cloves garlic
1 bunch cilantro, chopped
Juice of 2 limes, divided
30 to 35 medium shrimp, unpeeled,
    heads removed

4 cups diced watermelon, honey-
    dew, and cantaloupe melon
3 tablespoons sugar
1/2 cup finely chopped mint leaves
1 tablespoon rice wine vinegar
3 cups romaine lettuce, cut into
    wide strips

Grind chiles in a spice mill to form a powder (about 2 tablespoons). In a bowl,

continued

mix the chili powder, oil, salt, garlic, cilantro, and juice of 1 lime. Add shrimp and marinate for 2 to 3 hours. Combine melons, sugar, mint, juice of the other lime, and vinegar. Refrigerate at least 30 minutes. Prepare a hot grill. Remove shrimp from marinade. Grill shrimp about 3 minutes or until done. Set aside to cool. Line 4 plates with the lettuce; drain melons and place on top of lettuce, then top with shrimp.

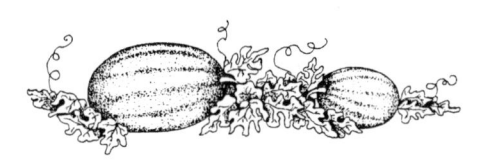

Cantaloupe-Avocado Salad

1 cantaloupe, cut into bite-sized pieces
2 avocados, sliced into bite-sized pieces
2 tablespoons undiluted frozen
    orange juice
1/4 cup lemon juice

2/3 cup salad oil
1/4 cup sugar
1 teaspoon salt
1 tablespoon grated onion
Pinch of pepper

Place cantaloupe and avocado pieces in a large bowl. Combine remaining ingredients to make dressing; shake well. Pour dressing over cantaloupe and avocado. Serve immediately.

Romaine and Walnut Salad

Cindy Manternach

Contributed by Cindy's sister, Kim Averkamp, Iowa City, Iowa.

4 cups torn romaine lettuce
2 plum tomatoes, sliced
1/2 cup sliced fresh mushrooms
1/4 cup chopped walnuts

1/4 cup red wine vinegar
6 tablespoons salad oil
2 tablespoons honey
1/4 teaspoon dry mustard

In a large salad bowl, toss lettuce, tomatoes, mushrooms, and walnuts. In a jar, combine the vinegar, oil, honey, and dry mustard. Cover and shake well. Pour over romaine mixture and serve. Serves 4.

Roasted Corn and Black Bean Salad

1 (1-pound) package frozen corn
    kernels, thawed
2 to 3 tablespoons oil
1 tablespoon salt
3/4 teaspoon cumin
6 tablespoons fresh lime juice
5 tablespoons oil
2 tablespoons cider vinegar
1 cup chopped fresh cilantro
1/2 cup chopped red onion

3 Italian plum tomatoes, chopped
2 jalapeño chiles, seeded, finely
    chopped
1 red bell pepper, chopped
2 teaspoons minced garlic
2 (15-ounce) cans black beans,
    drained and rinsed
2 large avocados, peeled, cut into
    1/2-inch pieces

continued

Heat oven to 450°. In a medium bowl, combine corn and oil. Toss to coat. Spread corn in ungreased 15 x 10 x 1-inch baking pan. Bake for 18 to 22 minutes or until corn begins to turn light golden brown, stirring every 5 to 10 minutes. Remove from oven and cool 10 minutes. In a jar with a tight-fitting lid, combine the salt, cumin, lime juice, oil, and vinegar. Shake until blended. In a large bowl, combine chopped cilantro, onion, tomatoes, chiles, bell pepper, garlic, beans, and the roasted corn. Mix well. Add dressing and stir. Add avocados; toss gently to combine. Serve immediately or refrigerate up to 6 hours. Serves 16.

Fiesta Pasta Salad

1 (12-ounce) package rotelle pasta, cooked, drained, and cooled
1 cup diced red onion
1 cup diced red pepper
1 (8-ounce) can of corn
1 (4-ounce) can diced green chiles

1 to 2 tablespoons diced jalapeños
1/4 cup chopped fresh cilantro or parsley
1 cup prepared Italian salad dressing
1 tablespoon chili powder
2 teaspoons ground cumin

In large bowl, combine pasta, onion, red pepper, corn, green chiles, jalapeños, and cilantro. In small bowl, whisk together dressing, chili powder, and cumin. Pour dressing over pasta mixture, tossing well. Chill at least 30 minutes to blend flavors. Serves 6.

Grapefruit Vinaigrette

An easy dressing for a fruit or green salad.

1 cup vegetable oil
3/4 cup grapefruit juice
1/4 cup lemon juice
1 tablespoon sugar
1 teaspoon salt

1 teaspoon paprika
1 teaspoon chopped onion
1/8 teaspoon ground pepper
1 clove garlic, cracked

Put all ingredients, except garlic, in a blender. Cover and blend for 15 seconds until smooth. Add garlic and chill for 1 hour before serving. Makes 2 cups of dressing.

—From *Fruits of the Desert,* by Sandal English

Chilis *and* Soups

Saguaro Cactus

Cream of Green Chile Soup

Carol Blakely

A modern version of a classic Sonoran soup.

4 tablespoons butter
3 (4-ounce) cans chopped green chiles
1 chopped onion
1 garlic clove, peeled and minced
1/2 teaspoon dried oregano, crumbled
2 bay leaves
4-1/2 cups chicken broth (homemade or canned)
2 medium potatoes, peeled and cut into thin pieces

1/2 teaspoon salt
1/4 teaspoon cumin
1/4 teaspoon black pepper
1/2 cup heavy cream
2 cups (about 8 ounces) grated Monterey Jack cheese
4 corn tortillas, cut into thin strips and fried until crisp

In a 4-quart saucepan, melt the butter over low heat. Add the chiles, onion, garlic, oregano, and bay leaves and cook, covered, stirring once or twice, for 10 minutes. Stir in the chicken broth, potatoes, salt, cumin, and black pepper and bring to a boil. Lower heat and simmer, partially covered, stirring once or twice, until the potatoes are very tender, about 20 minutes. Stir in the cream and adjust the seasoning if necessary.

The soup can be prepared up to 3 days ahead. Cool it completely and refrigerate, covered. Reheat it over low heat, stirring often. Ladle the soup into wide bowls, sprinkle the cheese over the soup, and scatter the tortilla strips over the cheese. Serve immediately.

Mexican Chicken Soup

1 pound skinless, boneless chicken
    breasts
1 cup coarsely chopped green pepper
2 teaspoons chili powder
1 teaspoon garlic powder
4 cups chicken broth

1-3/4 cups frozen whole kernel corn
1 cup cooked rice
1 teaspoon chopped fresh cilantro
    or parsley
5 lime wedges

Cut chicken into bite-sized cubes. Spray a large saucepan with cooking spray and warm over medium heat for a minute. Add chicken, pepper, chili powder, and garlic powder. Cook for 5 minutes or until chicken is done, stirring often. Add

broth, corn, and rice. Stir in cilantro. Simmer 10 minutes or until corn is cooked. Serve with lime wedges. Makes 5 bowls of soup.

Corn Pepper Chowder

8 cups cooked corn
1 cup water
3 cups chicken broth
2 cans evaporated milk

2 to 3 jalapeños, seeds removed,
  finely chopped
1 (7-ounce) jar roasted peppers

Blend 4 cups of the corn and the water in a blender until creamy. Pour into a large Dutch oven and add remaining ingredients, including reserved corn. Heat until almost boiling. Serves 6.

Endive Soup

Mary Jo Richmond

1 large head endive
2 tablespoons butter
3 eggs

1/2 cup grated Parmesan cheese
1 (46-ounce) can chicken broth

Cook endive in enough salted water to cover until tender. Drain well, then cut up endive. Melt butter in a large pan; add endive and cook about 3 minutes. Cool. Whisk the eggs together; combine eggs, endive, and cheese. Heat broth to boiling and add endive mixture. Cook 10 to 15 minutes. Freezes well. Serves 6.

Chili Blanco Especial

Mary Jo Richmond

1 pound dry white Northern beans
7 cups chicken broth, divided
2 cloves garlic, minced
1 large white onion, chopped
1 tablespoon ground white pepper
1 teaspoon salt
1 tablespoon dry oregano
1 tablespoon ground cumin
1/2 teaspoon ground cloves
1 (7-ounce) can diced green chiles

5 cups cooked chicken breast
1 tablespoon diced jalapeño chile
    (optional)
8 flour tortillas
1/2 cup shredded Monterey Jack
    cheese
1/2 cup sliced black olives
1 cup salsa
1/2 cup sour cream
1 avocado, diced

Soak beans in water to cover for 24 hours; drain. In a crockpot or large kettle, combine beans, 5-1/4 cups broth, garlic, onion, white pepper, salt, oregano, cumin, and cloves. Simmer, covered, for about 5 hours until beans are tender, stirring occasionally. Stir in green chiles, chicken, and remaining broth. For more heat, add the jalapeños. To serve, line 8 bowls with flour tortillas. Spoon in chili, then top with the following, as desired: shredded cheese, olives, salsa, sour cream, and diced avocado.

Green Chile Con Carne

1 teaspoon canola oil
1-1/2 to 2 pounds round steak, cut
    into bite-sized pieces
1/2 cup diced onion
1 teaspoon salt
1 tablespoon flour

1 medium tomato, diced
4 green chiles, roasted, peeled and
    diced
Dash of garlic powder
2 to 3 cups water

Heat oil in a large skillet over medium heat. Add steak pieces and brown. Mix in remaining ingredients and cook for 15 minutes over low heat, stirring occasionally. Add water depending on desired thickness. Simmer for 25 minutes. Serves 4.

Chili Con Carne

Some chili lovers say chili tastes best when made the day before and refrigerated overnight. Skim off the fat before reheating for a healthier meal.

1-1/2 pounds flank steak, cut into
    bite-sized pieces
1 cup flour
1/2 teaspoon cumin
1 teaspoon dried oregano
1/2 teaspoon thyme

2 to 4 tablespoons ground red chile,
    to taste
2 tablespoons oil
1/2 cup finely chopped onion
1 tablespoon minced garlic
4-1/2 cups boiling water
1 tablespoon masa harina

continued

Chili Con Carne *continued*

Dredge steak chunks in a mixture of flour, cumin, oregano, thyme, and red chile. Heat the oil in a large, heavy pot or Dutch oven; add the onion and garlic, cooking until tender. Add the meat and brown. Pour in the water and simmer until meat is tender, roughly 1-1/2 hours. Add the masa harina during the last half hour to thicken the chili, if desired. Serves 4.

Arizona Cookout

Whether it's a campfire or a cookout, many of these recipes are designed to get you out of the kitchen and into the out-of-doors.

San Francisco Peaks

Campfire Steaks

The night before a camping trip or cookout, marinate these steaks and seal tightly in a plastic bag.

4 rib-eye steaks, 1 inch thick
1/2 teaspoon olive oil
2 tablespoons white wine
2 tablespoons soy sauce

1 tablespoon minced garlic
1 teaspoon chopped green chiles or a
    dash of hot chile sauce

Combine all ingredients in a plastic bag. Seal tightly and marinate overnight. Grill steaks over medium-hot coals until done or cook in a heavy frying pan, about 5 to 7 minutes per side.

Honey Mustard Glazed Steaks

4 well-trimmed boneless beef top loin
    or rib-eye steaks, 1 inch thick
1/2 cup Dijon-style mustard
1 teaspoon oregano
1-1/2 tablespoons honey

1 tablespoon cider vinegar
1 tablespoon water
1/4 teaspoon hot chile sauce
1/2 teaspoon black pepper

Remove steaks from refrigerator and bring to room temperature. Combine all remaining ingredients and mix well. Coat the steaks with the glaze, reserving some for basting, and place on a grill over medium-hot coals. Grill, basting with glaze, until steaks are medium-rare to medium, about 12 to 15 minutes. Serves 4.

South of the Border Wrap

American Dairy Association, Dairy Council of Arizona, Inc.

Wraps are sandwiches with a twist—fillings wrapped in tortillas or other flat breads.

1/2 cup drained, canned black beans
2 tablespoons salsa
1 tablespoon chopped green onions
1 tablespoon chopped fresh cilantro

1 large tomato, chopped
1 cup shredded Monterey Jack cheese
4 (8-inch) flour tortillas
Butter, as needed

Mash beans slightly with a fork and combine with salsa, green onions, and cilantro. Divide mixture between the tortillas, then top each with chopped toma-

toes and cheese. Roll up tortilla. Melt butter in a large skillet and grill the wraps, seam side down, over medium heat for 5 minutes, turning to brown on all sides. Makes 4 wraps.

Summer Roll-Up

American Dairy Association, Arizona Dairy Council, Inc.

You can make these wraps a day ahead and refrigerate. Or, toss them in a cooler with ice and take them along for an elegant picnic.

1 pound (24 spears) asparagus
1 to 2 red bell peppers, roasted
4 sun-dried tomatoes

4 to 6 tablespoons herb cheese
    spread, at room temperature
8 to 10 (8-inch) flour tortillas

Trim asparagus tips to 4- to 5-inch lengths. In boiling salted water, cook asparagus tips until tender, about 5 minutes. Rinse under cold water, then dry thoroughly. Cut peppers into 1/2-inch-wide strips. Soak the sun-dried tomatoes in

boiling water for 10 minutes; drain and finely chop. Add the tomatoes to the herb cheese and mix well. Spread each tortilla with about 1 tablespoon of the cheese spread. Cut tortillas into 1-1/2-inch-wide strips. Place 1 asparagus tip and 1 pepper strip together at one end of a tortilla strip and tightly roll in a spiral. Repeat with remaining asparagus and peppers.

Honey Baked Onions

3 large red or yellow onions
1/4 cup water
1/3 cup honey
3 tablespoons melted butter or
    margarine

1 teaspoon paprika
1 teaspoon ground coriander
1/8 teaspoon cayenne pepper

Peel and cut onions in half crosswise. Place cut side down in a foil baking pan. Sprinkle with water and cover tightly with foil. Place over medium coals and cook for about half an hour, or bake in a shallow baking pan at 350° for 30 minutes. In a small bowl, combine remaining ingredients. Remove onions from heat and spoon

half the honey mixture over them. Return to heat for 15 minutes. Baste with remaining mixture and cook another 15 minutes or until the onions are tender.

Grilled Chicken with Peach Salsa

Salsa:

3 peaches

1/2 red bell pepper, finely chopped

1/3 cucumber, peeled, seeded, finely chopped

2 green onions

1 jalapeño, seeded, finely chopped

1 tablespoon honey

2 tablespoons lime juice

1 tablespoon finely chopped cilantro

Salt, to taste

Marinade:

3 tablespoons olive oil

2 tablespoons white wine

3 tablespoons lime juice

1 tablespoon garlic, minced

1 teaspoon finely chopped cilantro

Freshly ground black pepper

4 skinless, boneless chicken breasts

Combine all salsa ingredients in a bowl. Mix gently and refrigerate at least 4 hours, stirring occasionally. For the marinade, combine all marinade ingredients in a large bowl. Add chicken and turn to coat well. Cover tightly and refrigerate 2 to 4 hours. Heat a greased grill to medium-high. Remove chicken from marinade and grill, or broil in oven, until thoroughly cooked. To serve, slice chicken diagonally and top with peach salsa. Serves 4.

Grapevine

Cowboy Beans

3 cups dried pinto beans, washed
    and drained
1 ham hock
1 green bell pepper, finely chopped
1 onion, finely chopped

2 cloves garlic, finely minced
3 tablespoons vegetable oil
1 tablespoon dried oregano
Chopped jalapeños, to taste
Salt and pepper, to taste

Place beans in a large pot with a tight-fitting lid. Add enough water to cover the beans by 3 inches. Bring the beans to a full boil and boil for 1 minute. Remove from heat; cover and let stand 1 hour. Drain the beans, discarding cooking water. Rinse the beans well and wash the pot. Return beans to the pot and add enough

water to cover by an inch. Add the remaining ingredients and return beans to a boil. Reduce heat; cover and simmer for about 3 hours. Stir occasionally, adding water if beans appear to be too dry.

Hunter-Style Pot Roast

American Dairy Association, Dairy Association of Arizona, Inc.

2 tablespoons butter
2 to 2-1/2 pounds boneless pot roast,
    well trimmed
2 medium onions, thinly sliced
2 cups condensed beef broth
2 bay leaves

3 tablespoons flour
1-1/2 cups plain yogurt
1-1/2 tablespoons lemon juice
1-1/2 tablespoons prepared mustard
1 tablespoon sugar
1/4 teaspoon pepper

Melt butter in a large Dutch oven. Brown pot roast on both sides. Add onions, beef broth, and bay leaves. Cover and simmer for 2 to 2-1/2 hours or until meat

is tender. Transfer meat to a warm platter. Skim fat from pan juices and remove bay leaves. Stir flour into yogurt until smooth. Stir in lemon juice, mustard, sugar, and pepper. Stir yogurt mixture into pan juices. Bring to boiling over medium-high heat. Boil and stir 1 minute. Serve over meat. Serves 6.

Mexican-American Food

Mexican influence runs strong in Arizona, where hundreds of thousands of Arizonans claim Mexican descent. Bordering Arizona on the south, the northwestern Mexico state of Sonora has flavored Arizona cooking. With an emphasis on wheat, corn, chiles, and beans, it is sometimes hard to separate the threads of American-Indian and Mexican cooking. Both lead back to ancient times and rely on the bounty of the Southwest. See "Dips, Salsas, and Hot Stuff" for more recipes with a Mexican flair.

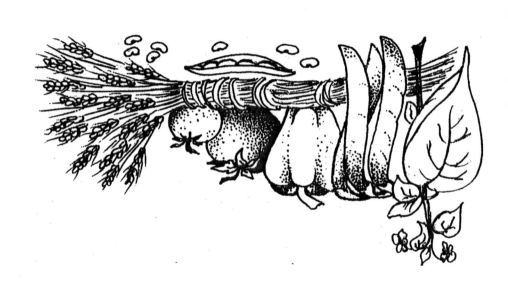

Chiltepin Chorizo

Carol Blakely

Chorizo is a hot, spicy sausage served with eggs for breakfast, as a filling for tostados and tacos, or mixed with refried beans. It usually is served crumbled.

1 pound ground lean pork
15 to 20 chiltepins, crushed*
1/2 cup red New Mexican chile
    powder
1 tablespoon chile seeds from
    chiltepins or other chiles
1/4 teaspoon salt

1/4 teaspoon freshly ground black
    pepper
1/2 teaspoon Mexican oregano
3 tablespoons white vinegar
4 cloves garlic, minced
1 teaspoon ground cloves

continued

Chiltepin Chorizo *continued*

Combine the pork with the rest of the ingredients, mix well, and let it sit at room temperature for 1 or 2 hours, or in the refrigerator overnight. (It keeps well in the refrigerator for up to a week. Chorizo can also be frozen and used in small portions as needed.) Fry the chorizo until it is well browned.

*The fiery hot chiltepin is the wild pepper that grows in the Sonoran desert of Southern Arizona and Northern Mexico. If you cannot find chiltepins, substitute jappones, pequins, or any other small, red, dried pepper.

● ● ● ● ● ● ● ● ● ● ● ● ● ● ● ● ● ● ●

Chimichangas

Carol Blakely

This Northern Mexican dish was made popular by the late Monica Flynn of El Charro in Tucson. It is now a standard menu item in Arizona restaurants.

3 tablespoons oil
1 medium onion, chopped
2 cups lean cooked beef or chicken
2 cloves garlic, minced
1 (4-ounce) can chopped green chiles
2 to 3 tablespoons chili powder
1/2 teaspoon cumin
Salt and pepper, to taste

4 tablespoons rice or red wine vinegar
6 flour tortillas
Oil, for deep frying
Salsa, to garnish
Sour cream, to garnish
Guacamole, to garnish
Shredded lettuce, on the side

continued

Heat oil in a heavy skillet. Add onion, meat, and garlic and cook until meat is warm and the onion is limp. Add green chiles, seasonings, and wine vinegar. Simmer until juices are cooked away, stirring often.

To make the chimichanga: Place 1/2 cup of the meat mixture in the center of a large flour tortilla. Fold the ends of the tortilla up toward the meat mixture, then fold the sides over the meat mixture. Secure with a toothpick. Deep fry in hot oil until golden brown. Drain on paper towels. Top each chimichanga with salsa, sour cream, and guacamole. Serve shredded lettuce on the side. Makes 6.

Breakfast Burritos

George and Linda Sayles
Olney House Bed and Breakfast, Safford, Arizona

1 onion, diced
1 small jalapeño pepper, finely diced
1 red sweet pepper, diced
1 small can kernel corn
1 ripe tomato, diced
2 tablespoons plus 1 teaspoon butter
    (plus more for frying)
1/4 cup salsa sauce

4 to 5 dashes Tabasco sauce
10 to 12 eggs
3 tablespoons water
1 teaspoon salt
Flour tortillas
Guacamole
Shredded cheese
Salsa

continued

Breakfast Burritos *continued*

Sauté onion, jalapeño, red pepper, corn, tomato, 2 tablespoons butter, and salsa sauce with Tabasco sauce until tender; set aside. Whisk eggs, water, salt, and 1 teaspoon butter and add to mixture. Cook until eggs are done. Brown tortillas on a griddle in butter on both sides, about 30 seconds. Spoon mixture onto tortillas and fold ends in to make a burro. Serve with guacamole, shredded cheese, and salsa.

Corn Tortillas

Corn tortillas are marvelously versatile and the backbone of many Mexican dishes. Fry them and break into pieces for chips, fold and fry for taco shells, or wrap them around meat or chicken for enchiladas.

1-1/2 cups cold water
1 cup flour
1/2 cup cornmeal

1/4 teaspoon salt
Vegetable oil, for frying

Thoroughly combine the water, flour, cornmeal, and salt. Pour 1/4 cup of batter into an 8-inch, lightly greased skillet heated on medium-low. Cook tortilla until dry around the edges, about 2 to 3 minutes. Flip and cook other side about 2

continued

minutes or until golden. You can use the tortillas for enchiladas or soft-shell tacos at this stage.

If you prefer crispy shells or chips, heat oil in a large saucepan to 400°. Drop tortilla in oil and bend almost in half with tongs to form a shell. Fry until golden and crispy. Drain on a paper towel. Makes 12 shells.

Huevos Rancheros
Claire Bourret

12 eggs, separated
2 (14-1/2-ounce) cans creamed corn
4 cups grated Cheddar cheese

1 (8-ounce) can green chiles, diced
1 tablespoon Worcestershire sauce
1/3 cup chopped parsley

Combine and stir all ingredients except egg whites in a large bowl. In a separate large bowl, beat the egg whites and fold them into the corn-egg mixture. Grease a 9 x 13-inch baking dish. Slowly pour mixture into dish. Bake 1 hour at 325° until brown on top. If it does not appear firm after an hour, bake up to another 15 minutes but do not over cook. Let stand 10 minutes before cutting into squares. Serves 10.

Mexican Casserole

Claire Bourret

1-1/2 pounds hamburger
1 medium, white onion, chopped
1 (16-ounce) can chopped tomatoes
1 (10-ounce) can enchilada sauce
1 teaspoon salt
1/4 teaspoon garlic powder
Pinch of black pepper
1 (3-ounce) can black olives, sliced

1/4 cup salad oil
8 corn tortillas
1 cup small curd cottage cheese
1 egg
1/2 pound Monterey Jack cheese,
    thinly sliced
1/2 cup grated Cheddar cheese
Tortilla chips

Brown meat and onion together in a large skillet. Add tomatoes, enchilada sauce, salt, garlic powder, and pepper. Drain olives and reserve liquid. Add olives to the skillet. In another skillet, heat the oil. Fry the 8 tortillas; remove to paper towels to drain. In a bowl, beat the cottage cheese and egg together. Line a 9 x 13-inch casserole dish with 4 of the tortillas. Spread half the meat sauce on top of the tortillas; spread half the cottage cheese mixture on top of the meat. Add half the Monterey Jack cheese on top. Repeat layering. Finish by sprinkling the Cheddar cheese over the casserole. Bake at 350° for 20 to 35 minutes. Add tortilla chips around the edges for decoration. Serves 6 to 8.

Beef Enchiladas

Variations on enchiladas are immense. They are usually a corn tortilla wrapped around a meat or cheese filling and topped with a sauce and cheese, then baked. You can purchase the sauce and tortillas to cut down on preparation time.

12 corn tortillas

Enchilada Sauce:

2-1/2 cups tomato sauce

1 cup water

2 teaspoons finely chopped onions

1 teaspoon salt

1-1/2 teaspoons garlic powder

Filling:

1-1/2 pounds lean ground beef

1 cup chopped onion

2 tablespoons flour

1/2 pound sharp Cheddar cheese, grated

Combine all enchilada sauce ingredients in a saucepan and simmer for 10 minutes, stirring occasionally. Remove from heat. For the filling, brown the meat and onions until onions are translucent and beef is no longer pink. Add the flour and stir. Add 1-1/2 cups of the enchilada sauce to the meat mixture and stir. Remove from heat. Dip the corn tortillas in the remaining enchilada sauce to soften. Lay a tortilla in a 9 x 13-inch baking dish and spoon 3 to 4 tablespoons of the meat mixture in the center of the tortilla. Top with 3 tablespoons of cheese, roll tightly, and place seam side down in the baking dish. When all enchiladas are assembled, top with remaining sauce and cheese. Bake at 350° for 25 to 30 minutes. Serve warm. Makes 12 enchiladas.

Tucson Tostadas

1/2 pound poblano chiles, or other mild chiles
3 medium flour tortillas
1/2 pound Oaxaca cheese, shredded

1/2 pound Monterey Jack cheese, shredded
1/3 pound Anejo cheese, grated
1/4 cup finely chopped coriander
Lard or oil, for frying

Preheat oven to 350°. If using fresh poblanos, roast them, and remove skins and seeds. If using canned chiles, wash and drain them. Thinly slice chiles. In a large frying pan, fry tortillas one at a time in lard or oil until golden brown. Remove to paper towel and drain well; place on a baking sheet to cool. Cover tortilla with

a thin layer of Oaxaca cheese, then with Monterey Jack cheese. Crumble the Anejo cheese over the other cheeses and sprinkle the coriander on top. Arrange the pepper slices on top of the tostadas. Bake for 5 minutes or until cheese is just melted. Remove from oven and cut into wedges to serve.

Burritos de Frijole

1 teaspoon shortening
2 cups cooked, mashed pinto beans
1/4 teaspoon garlic powder
6 flour tortillas

2 green onions, chopped
2 cups grated Cheddar cheese
4 to 8 tablespoons hot sauce

Heat shortening at medium temperature in a medium-sized skillet. Add beans and garlic powder, stirring until heated through. Place 1/3 cup of bean mixture on the bottom third of each tortilla; top with onions and 1/4 cup cheese and fold into thirds. Place burritos into a greased 1-1/2 quart casserole dish; sprinkle with hot sauce and remaining cheese. Bake at 350° for 15 minutes or until cheese melts. Makes 6.

Quesadilla

1 to 2 teaspoons cooking oil
2 (6-inch) flour tortillas
1/2 cup shredded Cheddar cheese, divided
1/2 cup cubed cooked chicken, pork, or beef

1/4 cup sliced, fresh mushrooms
1/2 cup shredded Monterey Jack cheese, divided
Sour cream and salsa

Heat oil in a nonstick skillet. Add 1 tortilla; layer with half the Cheddar cheese, then all of the chicken and mushrooms and half the Monterey Jack cheese. Top with the second tortilla. Cover and heat until cheese melts and the bottom tor-

continued

Quesadilla *continued*

tilla is crisp and golden brown. Turn over; cook until bottom tortilla is crisp and brown. Sprinkle remaining cheese on top. Remove from heat and cool slightly. Cut into wedges and serve with sour cream and salsa.

Lake Havasu State Park

Chicken Enchiladas

1 medium-sized onion, chopped
2 tablespoons margarine
1-1/2 cups shredded, cooked chicken
    or turkey
1-1/2 cups picanté sauce, divided

3 ounces cream cheese, cubed
1 teaspoon ground cumin
2 cups grated sharp Cheddar cheese,
    divided
8 flour tortillas

In a skillet, sauté the onion in margarine, stirring constantly until tender. Stir in chicken or turkey, 1/4 cup picanté sauce, cream cheese, and cumin. Cook until thoroughly heated. Stir in 1 cup of the Cheddar cheese. Remove from heat. Spoon about 1/3 cup of the chicken mixture in the center of each tortilla and

continued

Chicken Enchiladas *continued*

sprinkle with cheese. Roll up; place seam side down in a greased 9 x 13-inch baking dish. Top with remaining picanté sauce and Cheddar cheese. Bake at 350° for 15 minutes. Serves 4 to 6.

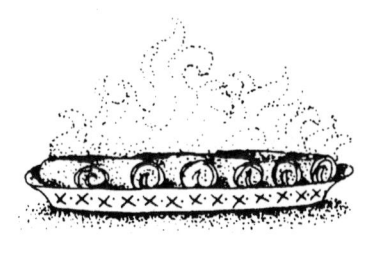

Tamale Bake

Topping:
1 cup yellow cornmeal
1 teaspoon salt
1 cup cold water
3 cups boiling water

Filling:
1-1/2 pounds hamburger or 3 cups
    shredded, cooked beef roast

1 cup chopped onion
2-1/2 teaspoons salt
4 teaspoons chili powder
2 cups canned tomatoes, chopped
1 (4-1/2-ounce) can black olives
1 cup grated Cheddar cheese

For the topping, combine cornmeal, salt, and cold water. In a large pot, boil

continued

the 3 cups of water and slowly add the cornmeal mixture. Cook, stirring, until thickened; continue cooking another 10 minutes. Spread into the bottom and on the sides of a 9 x 13-inch baking pan, reserving some of the mush to cover the top.

For the filling, brown the beef and onion. Drain any fat; return beef to the heat and add all other ingredients except the cheese. Simmer, covered, for 20 minutes. Remove from heat and spread over the corn mush. Top with reserved mush. Bake at 350° for 1 hour. Sprinkle with cheese and return to oven just until cheese melts. Serves 8 to 10.

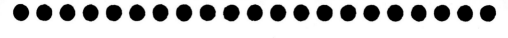

Chiles Rellenos Casserole

6 eggs, separated
1 pound Monterey Jack cheese, grated
8 ounces canned whole green chiles,
 or 12 fresh chiles, skinned

1 pound Colby Longhorn cheese,
 grated

Beat egg whites until stiff. In a separate bowl, beat the yolks until smooth. Fold the yolks into the whites. In a greased 9 x 13-inch pan, spread 1/3 of the egg mixture. Slit open the green chiles and place 4 on top of the egg mixture. Sprinkle 1/3 of the grated cheese on top. Repeat layers. Bake at 350° for 15 to 20 minutes.

Mexican Rice

3 tablespoons oil
1 cup uncooked rice
1/2 cup chopped onion
1 teaspoon minced garlic

1-1/2 cups tomato sauce
3 cups water
1/2 teaspoon salt

Heat oil in a large pan. Add rice, stirring constantly over medium heat until rice is golden brown. Add onion and minced garlic; cook until tender. Stir in tomato sauce and heat to boiling. Add water and salt and return to a boil. Cover and simmer 30 to 40 minutes or until all the liquid is gone. Serves 4.

Refried Beans

3 tablespoons lard or shortening
4 cups cooked pinto beans, mashed

1/2 cup Monterey Jack cheese, shredded

Heat lard or shortening in a large skillet. Add the mashed beans and cook, stirring constantly until thoroughly heated. Remove from heat and sprinkle with cheese. Serve warm. Serves 4.

Editor's Note: The "fat conscious" cook may eliminate the lard or shortening by heating the beans in a microwave oven.

Beef Tacos

1-1/2 pounds ground beef
1/2 cup diced onion
1 teaspoon oregano
1 teaspoon minced garlic
1 teaspoon salt
1/4 teaspoon pepper
1/2 teaspoon crushed cumin seeds

2 tablespoons ground chile
3/4 cup water
12 tortilla shells, warmed
2 cups chopped lettuce
2 fresh tomatoes, diced
2-1/2 cups grated cheese

Brown ground beef and drain. Add onions, oregano, and garlic. Cook until onions are tender; add salt, pepper, cumin seeds, ground chile, and water. Simmer 10 to 15 minutes. Place filling in warm tortilla shells and top with lettuce, tomatoes, and cheese. Makes 12 tacos.

Empanadas

Empanadas are simply turnovers. They can be baked or fried and filled with jams, cheese, or meat. This is a savory recipe; you can add bits of leftover meats or chiles to the filling or substitute your favorite cheese for the Monterey Jack.

4 cups flour

1 teaspoon salt

1-1/3 cups shortening or lard

Cold water

2 cups grated Monterey Jack cheese

Combine flour and salt. Cut in shortening and add just enough cold water to bind dough. Roll out about 1/8 inch thick and cut into about 2 dozen 3- to 4-inch rounds. Place 1 heaping tablespoon of cheese in the center of each round. Moisten edges with cold water; fold over, tightly sealing edges. Bake at 350° for 15 to 20 minutes until golden brown.

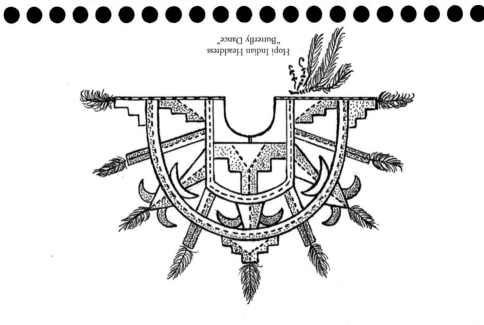

Hopi Indian Headdress
"Butterfly Dance"

●●●●●●●●●●●●●●●●●●●●●●●●●

American-Indian Food

... wild game, blue corn, beans, chiles, squash, pumpkins, prickly pears ...

Blue corn, gaining in popularity all over the country as a "New Age" food, has long been used by American Indians who favor its delicate taste over yellow or white corn. Many recipes calling for blue cornmeal also use ashes, which help maintain the blue coloring. If the ashes are omitted, the color can turn gray or even green. You may use blue cornmeal in any recipe calling for yellow or white cornmeal or vice versa.

Blue Corn Bread

Plant ashes, which impart color and minerals, are frequently used in American-Indian foods. For this recipe, burn the green part of the juniper, not the branch, until you collect enough ashes. You may skip the ashes but reduce the water to compensate for the omission.

1/2 cup juniper ashes   3 cups blue cornmeal
2-1/4 cups boiling water, divided

Mix ashes and 1/2 cup boiling water. Strain the mixture through a colander and set aside. In a pot, boil 1-3/4 cups of water. Add the juniper mix and stir. Add the blue cornmeal and stir. Cool. Knead the mixture until a soft, firm dough forms. Shape into a loaf and wrap in foil. Bake at 350° for an hour. Serve warm.

Mutton or Lamb Stew

You may use any cut of mutton or lamb for this Navajo staple. Neck bones, however, are most economical.

2 pounds mutton or lamb bones
6 cups water
3 medium potatoes, peeled and cut
    into bite-sized pieces
1 onion, diced

1 stalk of celery, without leaves, diced
3 roasted green chiles, peeled,
    seeded, and chopped
Salt, to taste

Place all ingredients in a heavy pot and bring to a boil. Simmer for 1-1/2 hours until done. Salt to taste. You may also add carrots, peas, squash, tomatoes, and corn to this stew. —From *Southwestern Indian Recipe Book*, by Zora Hesse

Navajo Corn and Cheese Pudding

2 cups corn kernels, scraped from cob
3/4 cup milk
1-1/2 cups yellow cornmeal
1/3 cup melted lard or shortening
2 eggs, well-beaten
1/2 teaspoon baking powder

2 roasted green chiles, peeled, seeded, and chopped
3/4 cup diced Cheddar cheese
1 teaspoon sugar
1/4 teaspoon salt

In a large mixing bowl combine corn and milk. Add cornmeal and lard and mix well. Add eggs and baking powder; thoroughly combine. Stir in chiles, cheese, sugar, and salt. Pour into ungreased 8 x 8-inch baking pan. Bake at 400° for 45 minutes. Serve warm.　　—From *Southwestern Indian Recipe Book*, by Zora Hesse

Pima Pinole

Add a few teaspoons of this mixture to milk or water for a nutritious drink, or add larger amounts of the mix to make a cereal. In the early days, honey and native spices were used instead of sugar and cinnamon.

1/2 cup blue cornmeal

1/2 teaspoon cinnamon

2 tablespoons sugar

In an ungreased frying pan, add blue cornmeal, stirring constantly over high heat until cornmeal begins to brown. Remove from heat and put into a jar. Add sugar and cinnamon and stir well. Cool. Cover jar and store until needed. You can substitute whole-wheat flour for the blue cornmeal.

—From *Southwestern Indian Recipe Book*, by Zora Hesse

Pima Baked Beans

2 cups pinto beans
7 cups water
1 cup diced bacon
1 onion, chopped

1/4 cup brown sugar
1/2 cup corn syrup
1/2 teaspoon salt

Sort and wash beans. Place in a large pot with water. Bring to a boil and simmer for 4 hours. Drain and set aside. In a skillet, fry the bacon. Add onions and fry until onions are soft. Add bacon and onions to the beans. Stir in the sugar and corn syrup. Add salt. Pour into an ungreased casserole dish and bake at 350° for 1 hour. —From *Southwestern Indian Recipe Book*, by Zora Hesse

Navajo Fry Bread

This is a good, basic fry bread recipe, although there is an infinite variety for this popular treat. Serve with beans, soups, or stews, or top with honey.

4 cups white flour	1-1/2 cups warm water
1 tablespoon baking powder	1 cup lard or shortening
1 teaspoon salt	

Combine flour, baking powder, and salt in a large mixing bowl. Add the water and knead until dough is soft and elastic and does not stick to the bowl. Add more water if necessary. Shape dough into balls the size of a small peach. Pat back and forth by hand until dough is 1/2 or 1/4 inch thick and round. Make a small

continued

hole in the center of each round. Melt the lard or shortening in a heavy frying pan. Carefully put in the rounds, one at a time. Brown both sides. Drain on paper towels and serve hot. Serves 6.

—From *Southwestern Indian Recipe Book*, by Zora Hesse

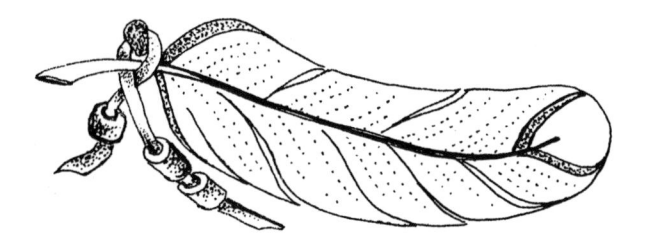

Tortillas de Harina

Joyce McCullough Peters

A Hispanic friend in Tucson gave this traditional flour tortilla recipe to Joyce.

2 cups white flour
Pinch of salt
1 teaspoon baking powder

3 tablespoons shortening
1/2 cup hot water
plus 2 tablespoons

Sift together dry ingredients; add shortening and work into flour mixture. Stir in water. Mix well, then knead and form into balls the size of an egg. Let stand for 15 minutes. Roll out on a floured board to about the size of a salad plate (6 to 7 inches). Place on hot, ungreased skillet or griddle on top of stove. Cook for about 2 minutes on one side; turn and cook for about 1 minute longer. Makes 12.

Blue Corn Tortillas

1-1/3 cups blue cornmeal   1 cup water
2/3 cup sifted flour

In a small mixing bowl, combine the cornmeal and flour. Gradually add the water and mix thoroughly. Divide dough into 12 small balls. Place balls, one at a time, between 2 sheets of muslin or waxed paper, or use a tortilla press. Roll out balls until they are very thin and about 6 inches in diameter. Fry tortillas over medium-high heat on a greased griddle or skillet. Flip to brown each side.

Fried Chiles

Chiles, especially popular with the Hopis, are a constant in many American-Indian dishes. This is a simple recipe using any green chile you have handy. Remember to remove the seeds and ribs for less heat. Always slip your hands into plastic bags or gloves before handling chiles.

12 chiles   Salt, to taste
3 tablespoons oil, for frying

Wash and dry chiles. Remove and discard stems. Slice chiles lengthwise into 1/8- to 1/4-inch sections. Heat oil in a frying pan over medium heat. Add the chiles and fry until crisp and brown. Salt to taste. Serve as an accompaniment to meat, eggs, or beans.

Desserts

Mission San Xavier del Bac
Southern Arizona

Mexican Wedding Cookies

American Dairy Association, Dairy Association of Tucson, Inc.

8 tablespoons butter, softened	1-1/4 cups all-purpose flour
1 cup powdered sugar, divided	1/8 teaspoon salt
1 teaspoon vanilla	1/2 teaspoon cinnamon
1 teaspoon grated orange rind	1/2 cup pine nuts, toasted, ground

Beat butter, 1/3 cup powdered sugar, vanilla, and orange rind in a medium bowl until fluffy. In a separate bowl, stir together the flour, salt, and cinnamon. Gradually add the flour mixture to the butter mixture, stirring well. Mix in pine nuts. Refrigerate dough until firm, 2 to 3 hours. Shape dough into crescents or roll into balls using about 2 rounded teaspoons of dough for each cookie. Place

continued

Mexican Wedding Cookies *continued*

1 inch apart on a greased cookie sheet. Bake at 350° until just lightly browned, about 12 to 15 minutes. Roll warm cookies in remaining powdered sugar and cool on wire racks. Makes about 2 dozen.

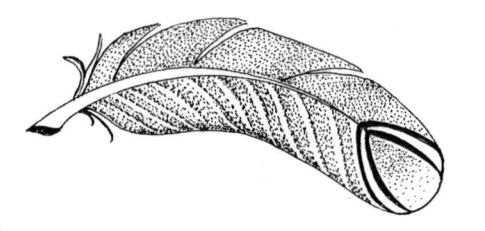

Flan

This delicious caramel custard is a Mexican treat loved throughout the Southwest.

1-3/4 cups sugar, divided
1 tablespoon water
3 egg whites

8 egg yolks
2 large cans evaporated milk
2 teaspoons vanilla

In a 9 x 9-inch pan, combine 1 cup of sugar and the water; put over heat. Stir constantly until sugar melts and is golden. Watch carefully so it doesn't get too dark or it will taste burned. Remove pan from heat and swirl until it is coated with the caramel. Let cool. For the custard, beat egg whites and yolks together in a bowl; add evaporated milk, remaining sugar, and vanilla. Beat well. Strain cus-

continued

tard into the caramel pan. Cover; place pan in a larger pan containing an inch of hot water and bake at 350° for an hour. While hot, turn custard onto a serving plate so caramel is on top. Cool completely; cover loosely and refrigerate at least 8 hours. Serves 8.

Arizona Apple Cake

American Dairy Association, Dairy Association of Tucson, Inc.

2 large apples, cored, peeled, cut
    into thin slices
3/4 cup sugar, divided
1/2 teaspoon ground cinnamon
1-1/2 cups all-purpose flour
2 teaspoons baking powder

1/2 teaspoon salt
1/4 teaspoon nutmeg
1/2 cup butter, melted
1/2 cup milk
1 egg

Toss apple slices with 1/4 cup sugar and the cinnamon; set aside. Combine flour, baking powder, salt, nutmeg, and remaining sugar in large mixing bowl. Add but-

continued

ter, milk, and egg; mix until well blended. Pour into well-greased 8-inch square baking pan. Arrange apple slices evenly over batter. Bake at 400° for 45 minutes or until a wooden pick inserted in the center comes out clean. Transfer pan to wire rack. Serve warm or at room temperature.

Lemon Ice Cream Pie

American Dairy Association, Dairy Association of Tucson, Inc.

You can make this pie with store-bought or homemade lemon ice cream.

3 egg whites, room temperature
1/4 teaspoon lemon extract
1/4 teaspoon cream of tartar
1/8 teaspoon salt
3/4 cup sugar
1 baked, 9-inch pie shell

1-1/2 quarts lemon ice cream
   (see page 129)
1 cup blueberries
1 cup raspberries
1-1/2 cups strawberry ice cream sauce

Prepare a meringue by beating egg whites, lemon extract, cream of tartar, and salt

continued

together in a large bowl until soft peaks form. For extra height, chill beaters in freezer before beating egg whites. Gradually add sugar, beating at high speed until soft peaks form. Spread meringue in pie shell, building up the sides. Bake at 275° until lightly browned and crisp, about 60 to 70 minutes. Cool on wire rack. At serving time, scoop lemon ice cream into pie shell and sprinkle with berries. Serve with the strawberry sauce on the side. Serves 8.

Lemon Ice Cream

1-1/2 quarts vanilla ice cream
   (slightly softened)
1/3 cup fresh lemon juice

1 tablespoon grated lemon rind
1/4 teaspoon ground nutmeg
2 to 3 drops yellow food coloring

Mix ice cream, lemon juice, lemon rind, and nutmeg in a medium bowl. Add food coloring to make a deep yellow color. Cover bowl with foil and freeze until ice cream is hard, about 8 hours.

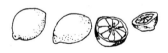

Pumpkin Cookies
Mary Jo Richmond

2/3 cup oil
1 cup sugar
1 egg
1 teaspoon vanilla
1 cup puréed pumpkin
2 cups flour
1/2 teaspoon salt

1 teaspoon baking powder
1 teaspoon baking soda
1 teaspoon pumpkin pie spice
1 teaspoon cinnamon
1/4 cup chopped nuts
1/4 cup raisins

In a medium mixing bowl, combine the oil, sugar, egg, and vanilla. Beat until fluffy. Add the pumpkin and beat until well blended. Combine the remaining

ingredients and gradually add to the batter. Drop by rounded teaspoonfuls onto a lightly greased cookie sheet. Bake at 350° for 10 to 12 minutes. Makes about 2 dozen cookies.

Fruit Leather

A great addition to a hiker's backpack—high in nutrients, taste, and convenience.

To make a fruit leather, purée any fruit, adding enough liquid to make a mixture thin enough to pour. Add sweetening to taste: either sugar or honey. Line a rimmed cookie sheet with plastic and pour the fruit purée onto the plastic. Dry in the sun, a dehydrator, or an oven until leather can be pulled away from the plastic. Sun drying takes at least a day, so protect the fruit from insects and bring the cookie sheet in at night. A dehydrator set at 120° takes about half a day. An oven set at 140° takes about 4 to 5 hours. When dried, roll up the leather in plastic and twist ends of plastic closed. Store in the refrigerator or freezer.

—From *Fruits of the Desert,* by Sandal English

Cactus Candy

Prickly pears are one of the best-known edible cacti. Some are yellow-green and some lean toward purple. Either variety works well with this recipe.

1 cup prickly pear juice
2 envelopes plain gelatin
1/2 cup water

2 cups sugar
1/8 teaspoon salt
Powdered sugar

To make prickly pear juice, place 7 or 8 washed prickly pears in a blender with 1 cup water and liquefy. Strain through layers of cheesecloth. To make candy, soften gelatin in water. Bring 1 cup prickly pear juice, sugar, and salt to a boil. Add gelatin and stir until dissolved. Boil slowly for 10 minutes. Pour into an 8-inch square pan and allow to set at least 12 hours. Cut into small squares. Roll in powdered sugar.

—From *Fruits of the Desert*, by Sandal English

Pecan Wafers

1 cup shortening
2 cups brown sugar
4 eggs
1 teaspoon salt

1 teaspoon vanilla
8 tablespoons flour
1 cup chopped pecans

Cream together shortening and brown sugar until fluffy. Add eggs one at a time; beat well. Add salt and vanilla; beat well. Stir in flour and nuts. On a greased cookie sheet, drop batter by teaspoonfuls, allowing 5 inches between, and flatten with a spatula. Bake at 325° for 10 to 12 minutes. Warm cookies may be shaped into rolls by wrapping around a thick wooden spoon handle or your finger, or cool flat on a wire rack. Tie cool rolled cookie with a thin ribbon for a festive touch. Makes about 6 dozen.

Pomegranate Jelly

Olney House Bed and Breakfast, Safford, Arizona

At the Olney House Bed and Breakfast, they make jelly from the seeds of pomegranates grown on their property.

3-1/2 cups pomegranate juice
1/4 cup lemon juice
1 (2-ounce) package powdered pectin

4-1/2 cups sugar
6 (8-ounce) jars with lids

To make pomegranate juice, juice 10 to 12 ripe pomegranates as you would an orange. Strain the juice through a cheesecloth-lined wire strainer. You may store

continued

the juice in the refrigerator for up to 5 days or you may freeze it. (Follow manufacturer's directions for sterilizing six 8-ounce jars for canning.) In a large kettle, combine the pomegranate juice, lemon juice, and pectin. Over high heat, bring to a rolling boil, stirring constantly. Add the sugar and stir. Bring to a second rolling boil and boil for exactly 2 minutes. Remove jelly from heat immediately when time is up. Let stand a minute to allow foam to form, then carefully skim off the foam. Pour hot jelly quickly into hot jars, filling jars to within 1/8 inch of tops. Carefully wipe off rim of jar. Put lid on each jar as it is filled, screwing band on tightly. Cool jars away from drafts on a towel. Jars will make a "tinking" sound as they seal. Store in a cool, dark place. Recipe fills 5 (8-ounce) jars with a little left for tasting.

Sopaipillas

This is a sweet version of a fry bread.

1 cup flour
1/2 teaspoon salt
1 teaspoon baking powder
1 tablespoon sugar
1/2 teaspoon shortening

5 tablespoons milk
Oil, for frying
Honey
Cinnamon and sugar

Sift together the flour, salt, baking powder, and sugar. Cut in shortening. Add milk to make a firm dough. Cover bowl and let rest about an hour. Roll dough about 1/8 inch thick on a lightly floured surface. Cut into triangles or rectangles.

continued

Sopaipillas *continued*

Heat oil to 375°. Fry only a few sopaipillas at a time to avoid overcrowding, turning frequently so they will puff. Fry until golden brown, about 2 minutes per side. Remove to paper towels to drain. Serve with honey or sprinkle with cinnamon and sugar. Makes about 12.

Cactus Wren
Arizona State Bird

Recipes from

Great Chefs of Tucson

Presented at the *Tables of Difference* Luncheon
for the Foodservice Consultants Society International's
Annual Conference, 1998
Tucson, Arizona

These recipes demonstrate the rich history of the Pimería Alta historic
region of Southern Arizona and Northwestern Mexico.

Enjoyed by Penfield editor Melinda Bradnan, who attended the conference.
Tables of Difference © *GourMedia & M.F. Munday, 1998*

Prickly Pear Crême Brulée Chimichanga

1 gallon heavy cream
1 pound sugar
1 vanilla bean, split
42 egg yolks
1 (2-pound) jar Prickly Pear Cactus
    Fruit Purée
24 (12-inch) flour tortillas

Additional Garnish Ingredients:
Crême Anglaise
Whipped cream
Cinnamon
Sugar
24 ounces diced avocado
48 ounces sweetened chocolate

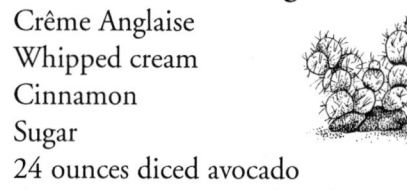

Scald cream, sugar, and vanilla. Add egg yolks, tempering them to mixture. (Temper in yolk to mixture by adding hot liquid to yolks slowly; add remainder to mixture.) Add prickly pear purée. Strain mixture. Pour into a 200 (12 x 20-

inch) pan. Place in a bain-marie (water bath), cooking in oven set at 250°. Cook until firm, but not golden. Cool and cut into 4 x 2-inch strips. Wrap in a flour tortilla and freeze. Take frozen, filled tortillas and fry at 375° until golden brown. Let stand in refrigerator for 30 minutes. Set atop Crème Anglaise on a plate. Top with whipped cream; sprinkle with cinnamon and granulated sugar and 1 ounce of finely diced avocado. Garnish with 2 ounces of broken chocolate bits. Yields 24.

—Bret Cirelli, Pastry Chef
Sheraton El Conquistador, Tucson, Arizona

Note: Whipping cream flavored with vanilla is a nice substitute for Crème Anglaise.

Braised Duck Legs with Red Cabbage

5 pounds trimmed duck legs
(thigh and drum)
1 pound mirepoix of vegetables
(onions, carrots, celery,
shallots, and garlic)
2 cups chestnut honey

1 cup raspberry vinegar
1 bouquet garni (parsley, thyme,
and bay leaf)
1 gallon de-fatted duck or
chicken stock

Render duck legs until golden brown on skin side. Add mirepoix and sweat until tender. Pour in honey and lightly caramelize. Add raspberry vinegar and bouquet garni, and cook to reduce vinegar by half. In a large roasting pan, place duck legs in stock; put in oven at 350° for 1 hour or until legs are tender. Remove legs and

reduce braising liquid by half to make sauce.

To prepare wilted cabbage, split and cut, as if for slaw, 1 head of red cabbage so that cabbage is in strips. Place in seasoned boiling water, or steamer, for only a minute or two until strips of cabbage are tender but not soft. Arrange legs, wilted cabbage, and whipped potatoes on plate. Pour sauce over legs when ready to serve. Yields 10 servings.

—Chef Christopher Cristiano
Wildflower, Tucson, Arizona

Black Pepper and Sesame Seared Ahi

Sesame Seared Ahi:
2 (5-ounce) ahi tuna blocks
2 tablespoons black pepper

2 tablespoons each, black and
    white sesame seeds
1 teaspoon kosher salt
Sesame oil, to sauté

Combine dry ingredients and roll ahi; sear in hot oil. Serve with beurre blanc (butter sauce) seasoned with fresh ginger, and marinated cucumber salad (recipe follows). Yields 1 to 2 servings.

Marinated Cucumber Salad:
2 cucumbers, diced
1/4 cup each: red, green, and yellow
    bell peppers
1/4 cup red onion, diced
1 tablespoon cilantro, chopped
1/4 cup diced poblano chiles

1 teaspoon each, black and white
    sesame seeds
1/4 cup white rice vinegar
    (unseasoned)
2 tablespoons mesquite honey
1/4 cup sesame oil

Combine all ingredients and let marinate for at least 2 hours.

—Chef Alan Sanchez
The Tack Room, Tucson, Arizona

Sweet Corn Boudin

12 large ears sweet corn,
   husked and kernels removed
3 red bell peppers, seeded and diced
4 Anaheim chiles, seeded and diced
3 cups diced tomato
3 tablespoons garlic
Salt and pepper

Olive oil, to coat
1-1/2 cups Crisco
3 cups cream cheese
1 cup heavy cream
16 egg yolks
Parchment paper and aluminum foil,
   as needed

Toss corn, peppers, chiles, tomatoes, garlic, salt, and pepper in olive oil. Roast in a 200 (12 x 20-inch) pan for 30 minutes at 350°. Whip Crisco in Robot Coup

(food processor) until it becomes light and airy; add the cream cheese and incorporate. Add cream and egg yolks to corn mixture; purée with Crisco to a fairly smooth consistency. Cover with parchment and foil and cover. Bake in bain-marie (water bath) for 1 hour at 350° or until set. Yields 24 servings.

—Janos Wilder, Chef and Proprietor
Janos, Tucson, Arizona

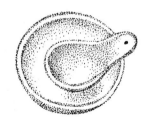

"Fuego Red" Beef Tenderloin Medallions with Sonoran Succotash

Sonoran Succotash:
8 fresh fava bean pods
2 ears fresh corn on the cob
1/2 cup roasted diced red
    bell peppers

2 sliced scallions
1/4 teaspoon unsalted Fuego
    Sonoran Seasoning
1 tablespoon unsalted butter
Salt and pepper, to taste

Split fava bean pods and remove beans. Blanch beans in boiling water for 1 minute. Shock in ice water; cool and drain. Peel outer shell of the fava bean away and discard. Roast whole ears of corn (yes, in husk) in a 375° oven for 45 min-

utes. Peel off husk and smoke for 20 minutes on outdoor grill with wet mesquite chips. Cool. Cut kernels away from the cob. Heat a large sauté pan; add butter and fava beans. Sauté beans slowly for several minutes; add corn, peppers, scallions, and seasonings. Sauté a minute or so until all ingredients are hot. Do not over cook as fresh appearance will diminish along with flavor. Serve with ostrich and beef medallions, or as a vegetable side dish.

Note: The complete line of Fuego seasonings may be purchased by contacting the Fuego Restaurant Bar & Grill in Tucson, Arizona.

continued

"Fuego Red" Beef Tenderloin Medallions:

1 tablespoon canola/olive oil blend

1 teaspoon unsalted Fuego
Red Seasoning

8 (2.5-ounce) beef tenderloin
medallions

1 teaspoon chopped shallots

2-1/2 ounces red wine

6 ounces diced smoked tomatoes

1 teaspoon tomato paste

1-1/2 cups beef broth

1 tablespoon ground walnuts

2 teaspoons chopped walnuts

1 tablespoon ancho chili paste

1 tablespoon freeze-dried corn

1 tablespoon fresh, chopped chives

1/2 cup chili-seasoned, roasted
walnut halves

Heat a large sauté pan until smoking hot; add oil. Season beef with "Fuego Red," salt and pepper, or your favorite seasoning salt. Place medallions in hot pan. Sauté a minute or so on each side, depending on thickness and preference. Remove beef medallions from pan and reserve. Pour off excess fat; deglaze pan with shallots and wine. Fashion sauce by stirring in smoked tomatoes, tomato paste, beef broth, ground and chopped walnuts, and ancho chili paste. Simmer until thickened, 4 to 6 minutes. Return medallions to simmering sauce briefly to coat. Arrange 2 medallions per portion on plate; top with sauce. Sprinkle with chives, corn, and chili-seasoned roasted walnuts. Yields 4 servings.

—Kent Pawlowski, Chef De Cuisine, Alan A. Zeman, CEC, AAC
Executive Chef/Owner
Fuego Restaurant Bar & Grill, Tucson, Arizona

Pork Carnitas Quesadillas with Mango-Chili Salsa

Carnitas:

2 pounds pork butt or pork
   tenderloin, roughly cut into
   1-inch cubes

3 cups water

4 cloves garlic, peeled

1/2 cup chopped white onion

1-1/2 teaspoons kosher salt

3 tablespoons chili powder

2 teaspoons ground cumin

1 tablespoon Mexican oregano
   leaves

1 stick cinnamon

1 tablespoon adobo from
   Chipotles

1 tablespoon tomato paste

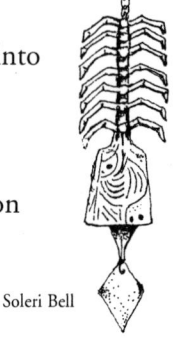

Soleri Bell

Place pork, water, garlic, onion, and salt into a saucepan. Bring to a mild simmer. Toast chili powder, cumin, and oregano in a dry skillet until fragrant and add to simmering meat. Add cinnamon stick, adobo, and tomato paste and simmer 1 hour. Add more water, if necessary, until all flavors are incorporated and pork is very tender. Increase heat to evaporate excess liquid. Remove cinnamon stick and shred meat by hand, with a fork, or with a food processor, and set aside.

Remaining Ingredients:

2 cups sautéed exotic mushrooms

2 cups grated Havarti cheese

2 cups cooked black beans

8 (10-inch) flour tortillas

continued

Pork Carnitas Quesadillas with Mango-Chili Salsa *continued*

Lay out the 8 tortillas and spread half of each with the carnitas, the mushrooms, cheese, and black beans. Fold in half and brown each side on a hot griddle. Place in oven to hold. Cut into 4 or 5 wedges to serve. Serve with mango-chili salsa (recipe follows). Yields 8 quesadillas.

Arcosanti
Paolo Soleri's experiment in self-
sufficient living, near Cordes Junction.

Mango-Chili Salsa:

2 mangos, peeled and diced
1/2 yellow bell pepper,
    seeded and diced
1/2 red bell pepper, seeded and diced
1/2 poblano chile, seeded and diced

1/2 jalapeño or serrano chile,
    seeded and finely chopped
1/4 cup chopped cilantro
2 tablespoons lime juice
Salt and pepper, to taste

Combine all ingredients; mix thoroughly and set aside in the refrigerator for at least 2 hours for the flavors to combine. Yields 3 cups.

—Matt Lash, Executive Chef, & Donna Nordin, Owner/Chef
Cafe Terra Cotta, Tucson, Arizona

Smoked Salmon Polenta Roll

1/2 teaspoon crushed garlic

1/4 cup diced onion

1/2 cup smoked salmon

1/4 cup water

3/4 ounce heavy cream

1/4 cup polenta

1/4 cup chopped tomato

1/8 cup chopped green onion

Salt, to taste

Parchment paper

Sauté garlic and onion until translucent. Add salmon and sauté briefly. Add liquids and bring to boil. Add polenta and continue cooking. When thick add tomatoes, green onions, and salt. Spread mixture evenly on parchment paper. Roll tightly and place in cooler to chill overnight. Unroll, slice, and serve drizzled with a walnut basil pesto.

—Michael Veres, Executive Chef
Daniel's Restaurant, Tucson, Arizona

Pork Loin Roast for Four
with Cinnamon Applesauce & Roasted Potatoes

Pork Loin Roast for Four:
2 pounds boneless pork loin roast
1 sprig rosemary
1 sprig thyme
1 clove garlic (reduced to paste)
Salt and pepper, to taste

Preheat oven to 500°. Rub roast with herbs and seasonings. Place in a roasting pan with fat side up and cook for 20 minutes. Reduce heat to 350° and cook for 30 to 40 minutes or until internal temperature is 160°. Continually baste roast with excess pork juices while cooking to maintain moistness.

continued

Cinnamon Applesauce for Four:

4 Golden Delicious apples   1/4 cup water

1 cinnamon stick   1/4 cup sugar

Peel and core apples; cut into medium-sized pieces. Add apples and cinnamon stick to water and sugar and bring to a boil. Reduce to a simmer for 15 to 20 minutes or until apples are very soft. Remove cinnamon stick and process apples through a food mill. Return to stove and simmer for another 5 minutes, adding water to desired consistency.

Herb Roasted Potatoes for Four:

4 Yukon Gold potatoes
1 tablespoon olive oil
1/2 tablespoon rosemary leaves
1/2 tablespoon fresh parsley

1/2 tablespoon fresh basil
1/2 tablespoon fresh chives
Salt and pepper, to taste

Preheat oven to 350°. Quarter potatoes lengthwise. Combine oil and herbs in mixing bowl and rub potatoes until evenly coated. Bake for 45 minutes or until soft when pierced with a fork.

—Peter Schmittman, Sous Chef
The Tack Room, Tucson, Arizona

Chevre Tart with Smoked Scallops and Maine Lobster

8 sheets phyllo dough

3 ounces clarified butter

3 whole eggs

3 egg yolks

10 ounces heavy cream

10 ounces half-and-half

1/4 cup roasted garlic

2 tablespoons chopped chives

1/2 teaspoon kosher salt

White pepper, to taste

6 ounces apple wood smoked scallops

6 ounces Maine lobster meat
   (knuckle and claw)

8 ounces Laura Chenel goat cheese

On a clean work surface, lay out phyllo and brush with clarified butter. Place another sheet on top and repeat process until you have 4 layers. With a steel cutter, or knife and round mold, cut 6 rounds large enough to fit the shape of a muffin tin. Place buttered phyllo rounds in muffin tins or other molds, crimping the

dough up along the sides. Repeat this process.

In a stainless steel bowl, make a custard mixture by whisking eggs and yolks; add cream, half-and-half, roasted garlic, chives, salt, and white pepper. Mix thoroughly.

Place 1/2 ounce of scallops and 1/2 ounce of lobster in the bottom of each phyllo dough-lined mold. Ladle in 2 ounces of egg custard mixture. Dot with goat cheese. Bake for 20 to 30 minutes or until custard has set and is golden on top. Remove from oven and cool, but do not refrigerate. Use within 1 hour. Yields 12.

—Albert Hall, Executive Chef
Hacienda del Sol, Tucson, Arizona

Ensalada de Lechugas Mixtas con El Charro Carne Seca

Carne Seca, an age-old southwestern specialty, is certified Angus beef, thinly sliced and marinated in a mixture of black pepper, salt, lime juice, and garlic. It is sun-dried in a high-hung outdoor cage, then reconstituted in a sauté with fresh green chiles, tomato, and onion. Carlotta Dunn Flores, in her book *El Charro Café: The Tastes and Traditions of Tucson,* suggests as a home method: Pull apart cooked beef. Dry in a 300° oven and reconstitute. To build El Charro's salad, the following is offered:

Mixed greens hand-tossed with El Charro's famous Carne Seca. The salad is lightly dressed with a spicy chipotle and garlic cream and served on a chalupa ("canoe"-shaped corn masa) bed, garnished with a fresh lime wedge and a sprinkling of *queso cotija* (dry, white, Mexican cheese).

—Candace Flores

El Charro Cafe, Tucson, Arizona

Arizona Sites

This is just a sampling of the many things to see and do in Arizona. For more information, call the Arizona Office of Tourism in Phoenix or visit them on the Internet at www.arizonaguide.com.

Alamo Lake State Park: Located 38 miles north of Wenden, this huge park hugs a 2,500-acre lake.

Arizona-Sonora Desert Museum: Located in Tucson. Learn about the flora and fauna of the magnificent Sonora Desert.

Bisbee: Ghost town known as Queen of the Mining Camps. A thriving copper mining town in the 1800s, it is now known for underground mine tours and the restored Copper Queen Hotel.

Canyon de Chelly National Monument: Just north of Window Rock are the canyons and prehistoric Anasazi ruins of Canyon de Chelly.

Casa Grande Ruins National Monument: At Coolidge are the preserved ruins of a Hohokam Indian structure.

Catalina State Park: A 5,000-acre desert park near Tucson offers equestrian services, hiking, picnicking, and camping.

Chiricahua National Monument: Spectacular rock formations in a pine forest near Willcox, 50 miles north of the Mexican border.

Colossal Cave: A large limestone cave, once a hiding place for American Indians and bandits, is a cool 70° retreat in Tucson.

Fort Huachuca: Now a museum, once an important army outpost.

Fort Verde State Historic Park: At Camp Verde, a museum and officers' homes show visitors how the base was crucial in calming the Apaches in the 1870s.

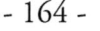

Four Corners Monument: Just east of Lake Powell, you can stand in four states at once if you straddle the monument marking the corners of Arizona, New Mexico, Colorado, and Utah.

Grand Canyon National Park: One of the seven Natural Wonders of the World. Hiking, tours, mule trips, and camping are available. Make reservations way ahead of time for this popular site.

Hoover Dam: Tour the highest concrete dam in the country.

Jerome: Restored copper mining town from 1876 is now an historical/arts center with a museum, ruins, shops, and restaurants.

Kitt Peak National Observatory: The Sonoran Desert southwest of Tucson is the spectacular setting for the National Optical Astronomical Observatories and the McMath solar telescope.

Lake Havasu State Park: Thirteen-thousand acres of recreational areas. The original London Bridge, brought to Arizona in 1968 when London outgrew it, spans the Colorado River here.

Lake Powell, Glen Canyon Dam, Rainbow Bridge National Monument: On the Arizona-Utah border, this 180-mile-long lake, hemmed in by the dam, features a natural rock span.

Meteor Crater: Resembling the moon's surface, this was once a training site for Apollo astronauts. A huge meteor left its mark more than 3 miles in circumference and 570 feet deep in northern Arizona between Flagstaff and Winslow.

Mission San Xavier del Bac: Just south of Tucson, one of the oldest Spanish missions in the Southwest, established in 1700.

Montezuma Castle National Monument: Ruins of the Sinagua Indian cliff dwellings at Camp Verde.

Mogollon Rim: In east-central Arizona is Apache country and home to the famous ponderosa pine forests that inspired Zane Grey's many novels.

Monument Valley: Colorful valley of eroded buttes provides the exquisite backdrop to many movies, television shows, and commercials. Hogan dwellings house sheep-tending Navajos. Hubbell Trading Post has operated on the Navajo Reservation since the 1870s. Fort Defiance was the set for the 1960s sitcom "F Troop."

Museum of Northern Arizona: Located in Flagstaff. Exhibits on the history of northern Arizona, plus Indian arts, crafts, and shows.

Navajo National Monument: Tonalea. Hike through canyons to the well-preserved Anasazi Indian ruins.

Nogales: Straddles the Mexican border. Popular for shopping and Mexican food.

Oak Creek Canyon, Sedona, Slide Rock State Park: Red rock canyon and home of an art colony in Sedona. Slide Rock has a natural water slide.

Old Tucson: Western movie set and amusement-park town.

Organ Pipe Cactus National Monument: Stunning Organ Pipe Cacti in the Sonoran Desert area of Ajo.

Petrified Forest National Park: In the Painted Desert, Indian ruins and the petrified remains of trees, plants, and dinosaur fossils.

Phoenix: Capital of Arizona and the fifth-largest city in the country features: Desert Botanical Garden; Phoenix Zoo; the Heard Museum, famous center for American Indian arts and crafts; Heritage Square, a 3-block glimpse into turn-of-the-century Phoenix; Phoenix Art Museum; Pioneer Arizona Living History Museum; Pueblo Grande Museum features exhibits on the Hohokam Indians; Arizona Science Center is a hands-on museum with a planetarium.

Picacho Peak State Park: Desert mountain park, 40 miles northwest of Tucson. A Civil War battle was fought here.

Prescott: Once the territorial capital, Prescott now boasts restored Victorian homes, the Sharlot Hall Museum, and Whiskey Row.

Saguaro National Park: Rich stands of these giant desert cacti are situated in Saguaro West in the Tucson Mountains, and Saguaro East in the Rincons.

Yuma Territorial Prison State Historic Park: Includes a 19th-century prison, the Century House Museum, and the Quartermaster Depot on the Colorado River.

American-Indian Reservations

More than 19 million acres of Arizona belong to the fourteen American-Indian tribes living there. Many Reservations have cultural centers and ceremonies open to the public. Before visiting, check with each Reservation so that you may respect their rules and customs.

Ak-Chin Reservation, South Valley

Camp Verde Reservation, Central Arizona

Cocopah East and West Reservation, Colorado River

Colorado River Reservation, Colorado River

Fort Apache, White Mountains

Fort McDowell Reservation, North Valley

Fort Mojave Reservation, Colorado River

Fort Yuma Reservation, Colorado River

Gila River Reservation, South Valley

Havasupai Reservation, Canyon High Country

Hopi Reservation, Route 66

Hualapai Reservation, Canyon High Country

Kaibab-Paiute Reservation, Canyon High Country

Navajo Reservation, Route 66

Tohono O'odham Reservation, Southeast Desert

Pascua-Yaqui Reservation, Southeast Desert

Salt River Reservation, North Valley

San Carlos Reservation, Superstitions

Tonto Apache Reservation, Rim Country

Yavapai Reservation, Central

Old Spanish mission at Tumacácori National Monument
was built about 1800.

Notes

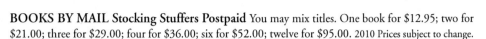

BOOKS BY MAIL Stocking Stuffers Postpaid

You may mix titles. One book for $12.95; two for $21.00; three for $29.00; four for $36.00; six for $52.00; twelve for $95.00. 2010 Prices subject to change.

Æbleskiver and More (Danish)
American Gothic Cookbook
Amish Mennonite Recipes
Buffets and Potlucks
Cherished Czech Recipes
Czech & Slovak Kolaches
   & Sweet Treats
Dandy Dutch Recipes
Dear Danish Recipes
Dutch Style Recipes
Fine Finnish Foods
Fire in the Bowl: Favorite Chili Recipes
French Recipes
German Style Recipes
Great German Recipes

Healthy Recipes
Microwave Recipes
Norwegian Centennial Recipes
Norwegian Recipes
Pleasing Polish Recipes
Quality Czech Mushroom Recipes
Quality Dumpling Recipes
Recipes from Ireland
Recipes from Old Mexico
Savory Scottish Recipes
Scandinavian Holiday Recipes
Scandinavian Smorgasbord Recipes
Scandinavian Sweet Treats
Scandinavian Style Fish and Seafood
Slavic Specialties

Slovak Recipes
Splendid Swedish Recipes
Tales from Texas Tables
Texas Cookoff
Time-Honored Norwegian Recipes
Ukrainian Recipes
Waffles, Flapjacks, Pancakes from
   Scandinavia and Around the World

License to Cook Series:
Alaska Style; Arizona Style;
Iowa Style; Italian Style;
Minnesota Style; Missouri Style;
New Mexico Style;
Oregon Style; Texas Style;
and Wisconsin Style

PENFIELD BOOKS, 215 BROWN STREET, IOWA CITY, IA 52245-5801 • 1-800-728-9998 • www.penfieldbooks.com

Grand Canyon